GRAPHIC AMERICANA
The Art and Technique of
Printed Ephemera

GRAPHIC
AMERICANA

THE ART
AND
TECHNIQUE
OF PRINTED
EPHEMERA
FROM ABECEDAIRES
TO
ZOETROPES

DALE ROYLANCE

PRINCETON UNIVERSITY
Library
Princeton, New Jersey
1992

ISBN-0-87811-036-4
Printed in the United States of America

PREFACE

Sixteen years ago in London, Maurice Rickards founded a society dedicated to the preservation and study of *ephemera* - the printed or handwritten documents of everyday life. This marked ephemera's introduction to popular culture as a distinct category of historic paper documents. In 1980, the nascent Ephemera Society of America organized the first conference and fair devoted exclusively to ephemera, and subsequent years saw the formation of societies in Canada, Australia and Austria. There are now hundreds of active members around the world, including many libraries, universities, colleges and historical societies; and last year a series of annual museum symposiums on ephemera was instituted by the American Society.

The Society is especially delighted to be a sponsor of Princeton's exhibition *Graphic Americana: The Art & Technique of Printed Ephemera*, the first major exhibit of ephemera at an American university. This volume, Dale Roylance's splendid catalogue of the show, beautifully outlines many of the various forms of ephemera, and is testimony to the value and significance of ephemera in the study of the graphic arts, social history, business history, and American studies in general.

Four Ephemera Society members in particular catalyzed and helped realize this exciting project: Jack Golden, a co-founder of the Society and an instrumental contributor to the Society's *Journals*; two Princeton graduates, Allen Scheuch and Paul Ingersoll, both ephemera enthusiasts and collectors; and Greg Smart, an ephemerist and co-designer of the striking exhibition poster. The Society is grateful to them, to William Joyce, head of Rare Books and Special Collections at Princeton, Dale Roylance, and the Princeton University Library, and to the many individuals whose enthusiasm and efforts made this project possible. We believe that this exhibit and catalogue will both broaden the understanding and appreciation of ephemera and encourage future exploration of the many facets of this fascinating genre.

William Frost Mobley, President
The Ephemera Society of America
April 2, 1992

INTRODUCTION

In both Latin and English, the word "ephemera" is defined as that which is short lived, or essentially transitory. In nature, the Ephemeron, or May Fly, is a common freshwater insect that survives for just one day. Similarly in printing - ordinarily "the art preservative of the arts" - ephemera is an unpublished class of throwaway printed paper artifacts characterized, like the May Fly, by a singularly short life span. Also much like the May Fly, printed ephemera may be seen as an aggregate swarm that usually defies both preservation and individual classification. For most of us, old printed scraps such as advertising cards, tickets, old programs and calendars are all temporary records, paper throwaways, useful as tinder for the fireplace. Yet from the beginnings of job printing of such ephemeral material, certain compulsive collectors have preserved these paper scraps as persuasive graphic witness to their times. Diarist Samuel Pepys was one of the first of such collectors in England. In America, printer Isaiah Thomas was the first great collector of printed ephemera.

It is a paradox that in our own time ephemeral paper accessories to daily life have come to permeate almost every aspect of living. Even our life records in the form of printed announcements and certificates of birth, graduation, marriage and death are, after all, only part of the larger mass of graphic ephemera. Similar kinds of printed records and graphic memorabilia were once a fascinating part of the essential etiquette, protocol and daily business of life in eighteenth and nineteenth century Europe and America. As such, printed ephemera is collectable history. It may be useful in understanding the full extent of this by grouping printed ephemera into six broad areas of association.

> *Social Ephemera*: birth, marriage and death announcements and certificates, stationery, calling cards, greeting cards, invitations, postcards and calendars.

> *Educational Ephemera*: book embellishments such as bookplates and bookmarks, rewards of merit, and diplomas.

> *Entertainment Ephemera*: posters, programs, playbills, tickets, playing cards and games, travel time-tables, luggage labels, World's Fair and circus memorabilia.

> *Military, medical, and civic Ephemera*: Insignia, draft and discharge papers, flags, badges and medals, recruitment posters. Medical and pharmaceutical, police and fire-fighting memorabilia.

> *Political Ephemera*: broadsides, campaign ribbons and buttons, flyers, and other patriotic regalia.

> *Merchandising Ephemera*: business and trade cards, salesman sample cards, advertising flyers, showcards, posters, labels, commercial advertising, and packaging, including wrappers, sacks, and boxes of all kinds.

As if all this were not pervasive enough in scope, the sweeping ephemeral nature of all of the above is exponentially being expanded in the present day. Quantity, however, has too often bypassed quality in terms of the graphic arts. The highly developed, often refined, printing techniques of the eighteenth and nineteenth century in engraving, woodcut, letterpress, and chromo-lithography, have been displaced, first by photomechanical printing, then offset lithography, and now by the electronic medium of a relentless commercial television. Through these new increasingly pervasive media two centuries of rich graphic arts development in early advertising printing arts may eventually be swept away, preserved only through the efforts of a new breed of collector, the ephemerist.

Our own collectors' choices of preserved ephemera, with selected examples of each category, are displayed in the multifaceted cards, prints and books of this Princeton exhibition. Many of these examples achieve a wonderfully democratic freedom of expression, as well as demonstrating remarkably skilled virtuosity of the printer's technique. Nearly all are from waste basket remnants of the previous century, here rescued and preserved as rare original examples of nearly lost printing arts. The exhibition and catalogue also attempt the seemingly impossible by giving preliminary classification of the species outlined above, and sorts out in alphabetical sequence, from *Abecedaires* to *Zoetropes*, the multifarious forms of printed ephemera, showing both new forms and imaginative printing developed by the many gifted, often anonymous job printers of early America.

Preparation of the catalogue was done on IBM and Macintosh computers, using Wordperfect and Microsoft Word, in Times Roman, by Agnes Sherman and Matthew Robb, Princeton Class of 1994. Clem Fiori provided the photography. Several collectors, including Paul Ingersoll, Princeton Class of 1950, Allen Scheuch, Princeton Class of 1976, Alfred Malpa, Jan Lilly, Joseph H. Felcone, and William H. Helfand have lent from their personal collections of printed ephemera. The Buccleuch Mansion Museum in New Brunswick, New Jersey, has provided the fine early New Jersey band box and the Trenton State Museum loaned the Paterson, New Jersey, watchpaper. Greatly appreciated financial help has been given by Jack Golden, Paul Ingersoll, and the American Ephemera Society. Jack Golden also designed the catalogue and opened up his remarkable collection to Princeton to enrich this highly selective overview of printed ephemera. Jack's guiding spirit, personal enthusiasm and knowledge continues to inspire us all with renewed respect for the arts of printing and design to be found in these all too nearly lost treasures of graphic ephemera.

Dale Roylance, Curator
Graphic Arts Collection
Princeton University Library

C.J. Fell & Brother, Philadelphia, chromolithograph, Herline and Co., no date. Graphic Arts Ephemera Collection.

Historical Introduction to
The Art and Technique of Printed Ephemera
Jack Golden

Ephemeral printing, in the form of single sheet broadsides, was a part of the first printing in the United States. While the first book was the Bay Psalm Book of 1640, Stephen Daye also printed an Almanac and a "Freeman's Oath" broadside, neither of which has survived - the way of most ephemera. A more famous early American broadside, "The Declaration of Independence," while rare, has survived as a national treasure. The American Press has thus produced ephemeral printing from the first.

By the mid-eighteenth century technological progress accelerated for the printing press along with the industrial growth of America. The onset of the Industrial Revolution in the mid-eighteenth century provided the commercial and industrial growth that concurrently initiated the phenomenal technological progress of the printing industry at the turn of the nineteenth century.

The first type foundry in America was established in 1796 by Binney and Ronaldson in Philadelphia. By 1812 there were three foundries, in 1839 sixteen, and by 1860 there were thirty-two, and more to come. Printers could now buy type whenever and as much as they wanted. Stereotyping was introduced in 1813. The iron hand press came into use in 1817. In twenty years the wooden press, in existence since Gutenberg, was to become extinct. Age-old paper making by hand also now gave way to the introduction of cylinder and Fourdrinier paper machines, providing the unlimited quantities of paper necessitated by the higher speeds of the new jobbing presses that developed in the 1840s and 50s.

The mail-order catalogue created a genre all its own with the introduction by the printing industry of new techniques of design, production expertise, quality control, and highly efficient mailing capabilities, all essential to mail-order success. Both job printed ephemera and the mail order catalogues of the nineteenth century reveal transformations of style and taste. Type specimen books were published that graphically demonstrate these changes. One in particular, *The Typograph, or Book of Specimens,* was published in 1870 by Oscar H. Harpel, a type designer and printer in Cincinnati. About 3,000 copies were printed, requiring, for its time, a phenomenal 476,000 impressions for the 264 pages (Fig.3). Most impressive by any standard, it reproduces hundreds of examples of contemporary letterpress printing submitted by printers from all over the United States.

From its inception in 1796, the invention of lithography by Aloys Senefelder opened up invaluable new vistas in graphic representation. One such capability, the simulation of copperplate engraving, became very popular for use in billheads, business cards, stocks and bonds. The gradual introduction of chromo-lithography, providing magnificent full color reproduction, enlarged the scope of the printing industry as never before. Although lithography was only introduced in the United States in 1821, by 1860 there were fifty-three lithographic plants, and by 1890 there were over 700. Although Currier & Ives are best known for their popular prints, (in their own words, "the very cheapest and most popular pictures in the world"), most of which were hand-colored, they did produce chromo-advertising posters and many advertising trade cards. Although other lithographers also produced "popular prints," chromolithography became the process of choice for advertising and publishing. Peter S. Duval (Fig.2), Sarony & Major, Hatch and Co., A. Hoen, Louis Prang, Bufford, Strobridge & Co., were among the many excellent workers in the new technique who established American lithography as some of the best in the world.

To achieve full-color chromolithography required the use of as few as five or six lithographic stones and, depending on desired effects and reproduction of specific colors, as many as twenty or more stones. Color reproduction today is achieved by the use of 4-color separation through the use of filters that separate original colored art into the three primary colors (red, yellow and blue) plus black. Lithographers, however, had to develop an expertise for determining the precise number of stones (one for each color) to be required, and what effects were to be expected with the overprinting of one or more colors. Remarkable accomplishments, truly to be admired, from an era primitive compared to the technologies of our time.

The invention of the halftone by Frederick R. Ives in 1878 was another revolutionary development in the history of printing. Black and white halftones came into general use by 1885. With the development of two and three color process through the early 1900s to four-color process in the 1920s, came the demise of chromo-lithography and an end to a magnificent, too little appreciated, era of fine original American color printing.

Figure 1. Engraved trade cards as advertisements in Joshua Shaw's *United States Directory*, Philadelphia, 1822. Lent by Jack Golden.

Figure 2. Chromolithograph Trade Card by Peter Duval. Lent by Jack Golden.

Figure 3. One of the folded color woodcut inserts in Harpel's *Typograph*, Cincinnati, 1870. Graphic Arts Collection.

Wall Calendar, chromolithograph with rotating pointer, Styles & Cash. New York, 1887. Lent by Jack Golden.

ALMANACS AND CALENDARS

Few things are discarded more rapidly than last year's calendar, and they may even be regarded, next to clocks, as the perfect graphic emblem of the ephemeral passage of time, day by day, year by year. The venerable ancestor of the calendar was the "Almanack" which in turn dates back to the Middle Ages with the *Ephemerides* of Regiomantus. The "Almanack" was part of the first printing in America. No copy survives (being ephemera), but an "Almanack" was published in Cambridge a year before the Bay Psalm Book of 1640. The American Almanac would become in the next two centuries one of the practical necessities of nearly every early American household, giving the days

Pool room calendar,
chromolithograph, artist unknown.
Lowell, Massachusetts, 1908. Lent by
Jack Golden.

Marchbanks Press Almanac,
letterpress, designed by Thomas
Maitland Cleland. New York, 1924.
Princeton Graphic Arts Collection.

of the months, the Zodiac, seasonal predictions, and much useful advice.
By the turn of our own century, however, the calendar came of age. Calendar
art began to take on far more urbanity with a new perennial favorite, the well
formed cover girl. Early versions of this may be seen in these examples of
1908 and 1924; ever more lightly clad models led to the pinup favorites of the
second World War. While the almanac form remains durably old fashioned,
(the Old Farmer's Almanack is still published) calendars are, like clocks, the
prevailing timekeepers in all our lives. "Calendar art" is now either highly sentimental or slyly erotic, both ways of momentarily escaping the urgency of time.

Geburts und Tausschein, hand colored woodcut, H. Ebner. Allentown, Pennsylvania, circa 1825. Graphic Arts Ephemera Collection.

ANNOUNCEMENTS

Announcements, in their larger printed forms, become *BROADSIDES* and *POSTERS* (q.v.) But there are also many miniature card announcements that were very important to the social order and etiquette of early American life. These were birth and death announcements that create distinct graphic symbols of the most meaningful of personal ephemera, our life records. Birth, marriage, graduation and death also have *CERTIFICATES* (q.v.) but these are formal, far less decorative records of these events. Pennsylvania-German printers evolved a particularly attractive pictorial birth record, seen here with woodcut angels welcoming a new arrival in 1825.

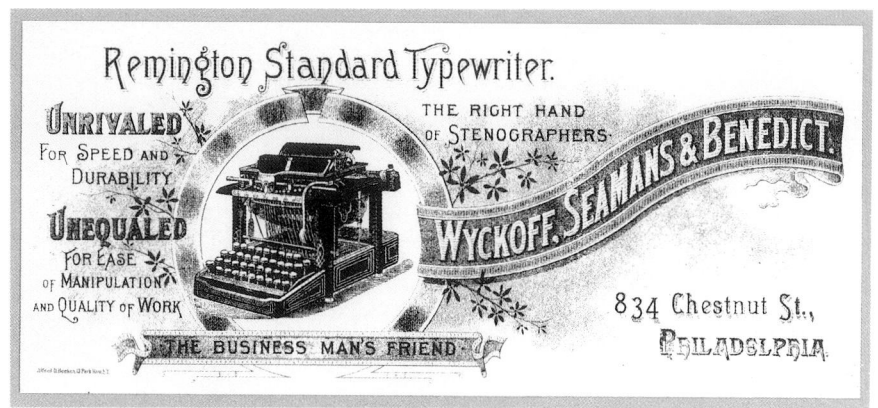

Selected Printed blotters.   Lent by Jack Golden.

BLOTTERS

Coarse, unsized paper to soak up wet ink is described as early as 1519 in W. Horman's *Vulgaria*: "Blotting papyr serveth to drye weete wryttynge, lest there be made blottis or blurres" (Labarre). By the early 19th century blotting paper was a characteristic pink color resulting from unbleachable red cotton rags, so that most of the earliest surviving blotters are of this color. Blotters, since they are saved until they are used up, are slightly less ephemeral as printed advertising surfaces, and on the blotting side left convenient clues for clever detectives from Sherlock Holmes on.

15

Early American binders' tickets, letterpress, printer unknown. Boston and Princeton, 1840-60. Collected by P.J. Conkwright, lent by Jan Lilly.

BOOK EPHEMERA - BINDERS' TICKETS

Ephemeral additions to the printed book include such bibliophilic amenities as binders' and booksellers' tickets, book marks, and bookplates. All might be described as paper furniture for books, added later to the otherwise finished book by the binder, seller or owner of the book. Good examples of such graphic garnishes are *BINDERS' TICKETS* which survive from that golden age when hand-bound books were a part of every gentleman's library, and leather hand binding a flourishing trade. Minuscule paper labels with the binder's name and address were pasted in as obscure a corner as the endpapers as the modest binder could find. Similarly discreet labels of the bookseller may also be found in many 18th and early 19th century editions.

BOOKMARKS

Bookmarks have their own curious history. One of the earliest forms of the bookmark may be found in medieval manuscripts and incunabula as small tabs of attached vellum. The indent mark of the modern dictionary is a modern vestige of that idea. Loose bookmarks are a later development, best represented by the many surviving fancy Victorian bookmarks made up from hand- or machine- stitched ribbons. Such bookmarks, as might be expected, became a standard accessory to reading, and were truly elaborate, often richly styled book adornments - useful as badges of cultural status, as well as literally keeping one's place. The bookmark has become almost a non-entity in our own casual reading day, since most any old insert or turned down corner or "dog-ear" seems to do the job. The more respectful, cozy gentility of Victorian bookmarks, like much Victorian poetry, alas, seems long past. The cloth weaving technique used for many Victorian bookmarks is also of special interest for its incorporation of an invention called the Jacquard loom, which first introduced a very modern idea: the programming of a machine to perform in a preset pattern. It was an idea that would lead to the computer. Such elaborately machine stitched silk bookmarks, now called Stevengraphs, were invented by Thomas Stevens of Coventry, England. They later became a specialty of the textile mills of Paterson, New Jersey, which in the 1880's was known as "Silk City, U.S.A."

Bookmarks, stitched silk "Stevengraphs," artist unknown. Coventry, England and Paterson, New Jersey, ca. 1880. Graphic Arts Ephemera Collection.

Early American engraved bookplates. Graphic Arts Ephemera Collection.

Ex Libris, Princeton University Library, printed bookplates. Princeton, New Jersey. Graphic Arts Bookplate Collection.

BOOKPLATES

The *BOOKPLATE*, by far the largest category of book ephemera, is a study in itself. Like bookmarks, the personal use of bookplates, or Ex Libris, is now little observed. This is unfortunate, since the interest and information to be discovered in old bookplates can be rewarding in several areas, including the history of graphic styles, from the 15th to the 20th century, often beautifully traced in these diminutive ownership labels. Gothic, renaissance, mannerist, baroque, rococo, art-nouveau, art-deco, as well as modernism, may be found clearly reflected in the historical design of five centuries of bookplates. The eighteenth century American heraldic plates shown here, for example, show Jacobean and Chippendale tastes as clearly as the furniture styles of the day. Their ownership is also of great interest. The plate of the early American printer Isaiah Thomas, the first great collector of American ephemera, as well as founder of the American Antiquarian Society in Worcester, Massachusetts, is shown here. Henry Dawkins, also shown, was an early Philadelphia engraver who made the first important view of Nassau Hall at Princeton.

Printmaking techniques-woodcut, intaglio, and lithography-make their clear chronological progression in bookplates as well. For collectors and librarians, the invaluable information of the provenance, or history of successive ownership, is often established by the various bookplates pasted on the inside front cover. Security against theft is also enhanced, particularly for most institutional libraries. Ex Libris of the Princeton University Library include the oval first plate, the wood engraved early nineteenth century plate, the etched late nineteenth century plate by Edwin French, and the current plate designed by Reynolds Stone.

19

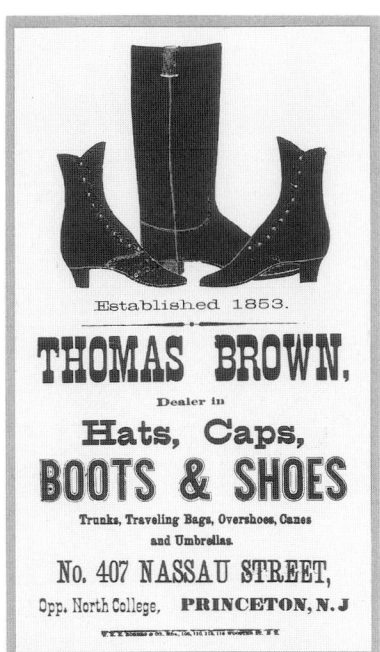

Early American Broadsides, including
Thomas Brown Haberdashery, woodcut,
W.H.H. Rogers. Princeton, New Jersey,
ca. 1850. Graphic Arts, Sinclair
Hamilton Collection.

*Troy, Ballston, and Saratoga Coaching
Broadside*, woodcut, J.H. Hall. Troy,
New York, 1834. Lent by Jack Golden.

BROADSIDES AND POSTERS

Perhaps the most expansive of all classes of ephemera is the printed single sheet
street literature known as the *BROADSIDE*. Broadsides perform as posted
announcements of every sort, from Royal proclamations, decrees and official
notices to FOR SALE, and WANTED notices. Like book formats, broadsides
may be folio, quarto, or octavo in size. Later broadsides also incorporated a
new printing hucksterism with the design and expansive use of new display
type faces cut in wood. These wildly inventive fonts of Victorian type design
departed dramatically from the dignity and formalism of earlier book
typography. As the nineteenth century broadside developed, so did an excess
of vulgarity in eye-catching manipulation of the printed alphabet. Types
described as "Egyptian," "Fat-Face," and "Grotesque" became commonplace
and the conventional broadside became that late 19th century ubiquity, the
pictorial poster. Typography, or printing layout, became ever more riotous
along with increasing emphasis on pictures. From the simple visual exuberance
of the 1850's later posters devolved into an orgy of chaotic and garish printing
best, or worst, witnessed in the barnside circus and patent medicine posters of
the late nineteenth century. Certain artists in Europe and America changed all
this, however, with their recognition of the potential of the poster as art. Cheret
and Toulouse-Lautrec in France, and Bradley and Penfield in America created a
newly simplified style for the poster, and gave new distinction to the emerging
profession of graphic design.

Selected Brochures. Lent by Jack Golden.

BROCHURES

The rotary press, which took the place of the far slower flatbed press in the late 1860s, made possible the vast expansion of the size of the printed edition. This, along with the development of two and three color printing and the simple economy of paper offcuts in smaller sizes, created a surge of advertising brochures, booklets, leaflets, and pamphlets. Large in edition but usually small in format, such printings were first sewn (*brochure* is derived from French *brocher*, to sew) and, much later, stapled. Early advertising brochures are also good examples of the soft sell, often pretending to be of didactic or cultural interest but still selling the image of the product. It is an idea prevalent today: the not-so-subtle promotion of the sponsor as cultural patron.

Selected calling cards and business cards. Lent by Jack Golden.

Selected calling cards and business cards. Graphic Arts Ephemera Collection.

CALLING CARDS AND BUSINESS CARDS

Early tradesmen quickly discovered the value of a printed name and address card. Many printers and engravers outdid themselves creating elegant examples of their craft. Once a well-mannered essential to social identity, the 4 1/2 " x 2 1/2" wallet size calling card, or *carte de visite*, solved many problems of social and business etiquette. Instead of awkward messages on a telephone answering machine, callers left their card, with or without written message, in an incredibly elaborate ritual of social protocol. They later included, in these inventive days of early photography, an actual tintype or albumen print of their own portrait. The fashion coincided with the Civil War, so that many *carte de visite* photos of Union and Confederate men exist as poignant graphic memorials to the many who did not survive the war. Like these images of vanquished young soldiers, many calling cards have a ghostly quality for the imagination, calling up long departed people and places with this one last surviving touch of printed reality. These early photographic cards are also the beginning of a rising floodtide of photographic ephemera not pursued in this catalogue.

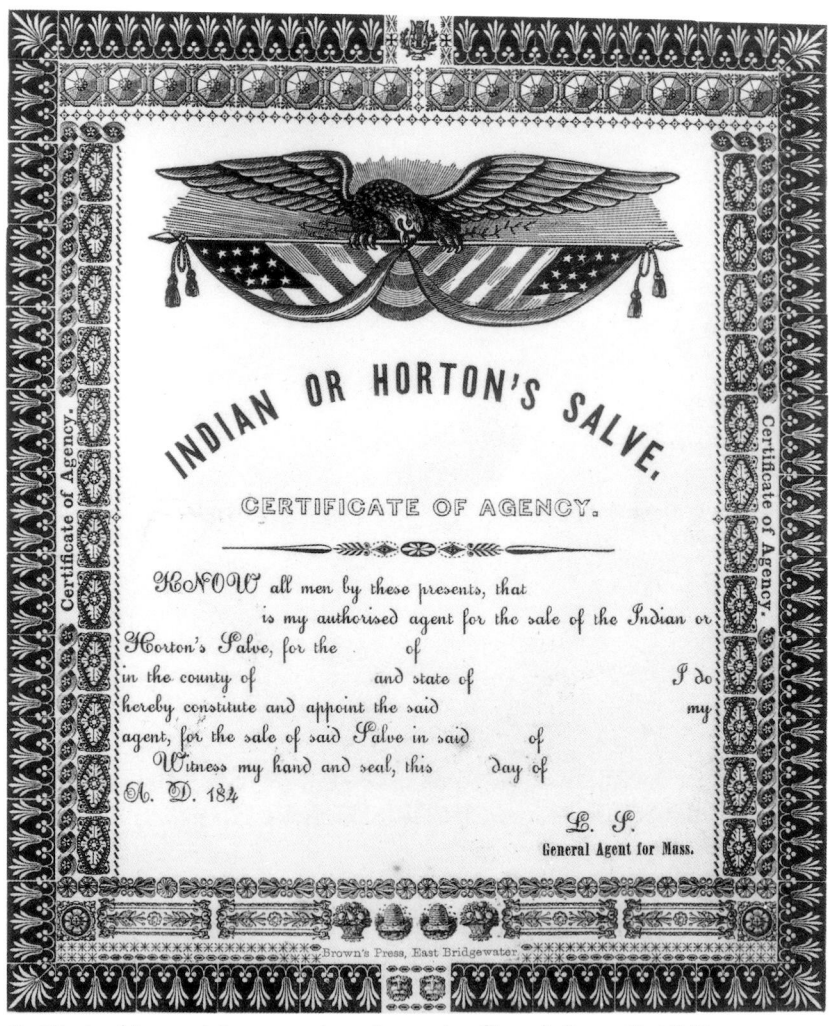

Certificate of Agency, letterpress and wood engraving, Brown's Press. East Bridgewater, Massachusetts, ca. 1840. Lent by Jack Golden.

CERTIFICATES

Announcements and certificates serve the purpose of printed record of important life events, and the certificate seems to make it legal. Many certificates thus acquire an importance beyond the ephemeral and may be zealously preserved as official record. Pseudo-certificates may also take on airs of graphic pretensions. This certificate of Indian ointment, printed up with regal rows of ornament, calligraphic type, and flag-draped eagle headpiece, is still only a dubious ointment claim. Birth, marriage and death certificates as well as diplomas, should signify almost the opposite of ephemeral, since they mark the most important of our life events. Brave efforts to make these events less ephemeral than they eventually are include bronzed baby shoes, picture albums, certificate frames, and tombstones.

Selected Dance Cards. Graphic Arts Ephemera Collection.

DANCE CARDS

These printed tokens of personal social success are rarely saved except by the most nostalgic of ladies or the most diligent of historical societies. Still, old dance cards have their place as graphic witness to such once important but now vanished social events as Summer Hops at West Point and the Firemen's Annual Ball, once held in towns across America.

Valentines, artists unknown. N.p, n.d. Graphic Arts Ephemera Collection.

DECOUPAGE

The invention of the die cut, which stamped out both embossing and the cut out image by machine, led Victorian entrepreneurs to develop a delightful new embellishment of the chromolithograph to all kinds of decorative uses. Known in England as "scraps", in Germany as *Glanzbilder* , and in France as *decoupage*, these colorful cutouts lent themselves beautifully to homemade valentines, Christmas greetings and scrapbook fillers. They were issued in diecut chromolithographed sheets, beautifully embossed, and helped make the fortunes of certain printing firms, most notably Raphael Tuck and Sons in London and Louis Prang in Boston. A far more sophisticated use of the idea of cut and paste *decoupage* has been a modern art development of *collage* by such high art painters as Kurt Schwitters, Pablo Picasso, Robert Motherwell, and Robert Rauschenberg.

Tinsel Print, engraving with die cut embossments on silverfoil, artist unknown. N.p, n.d. Graphic Arts Ephemera Collection.

EMBOSSMENTS

Closely related to decoupage is the printing principle of embossment or blind stamp printing. It was and is appreciated for its elegance of effect both in the East, where the effect is now known as *gauffrage* in Japanese prints, and in the West where it is best described as inkless intaglio. It is the paper equivalent of bas-relief and cameo jewelry, expensive to create and a sure way to suggest elegance in graphic design. Gilt embossments were also cut up and pasted on engravings as delightful homemade pictures called "Tinsel Prints" in the early nineteenth century.

Bonnet Styles, color lithograph, Kohn, Adler & Co. Philadelphia, 1880. Lent by Jack Golden.

FANS

The folding fan is a too-little-appreciated example of inspired simplicity in early folded paper engineering. Pleated leaves of paper parchment, or silk, are attached to a rivet or pin, which unfold to become both highly decorative and personal breeze maker. Folding fans date from the Ming period in China and were brought to Europe early in the sixteenth century by Portuguese traders. Both the folding fan and the ancient flat, palmate fan were adapted to advertising purposes in America in the late nineteenth century. Such printed fans were highly democratic versions of the aristocratic ladies fans that were so essential as an accessory of etiquette and fashionable dress in the century before.

Quarterly Report of Ladies Fashions, chromolithograph, Louis Maurer. New York, 1875. Lent by Jack Golden.

FASHION PLATES

By definition, fashion design changes with the season. The history of these changes is beautifully recorded in printed fashion plates, both for advertising and for at home pattern users. Gift Book Annuals, *Peterson's*, and *Godey's Ladies Book*, with their hand colored plates and patterns, became enormously popular. The history of taste and social attitudes are also very well documented here, as are the graphic techniques used to print such plates, usually in the best and latest printing technique. Some of the best color lithography of the nineteenth century is to be found in late Victorian fashion posters, just as the finest *pochoir*, or paint stencilled printing, was the vogue for fashion plates of the Art Deco period.

A SUPERANNUATED
HORTICULTURIST.

"VOILÀ !"

Harlequin playing cards, design by Charles Carryl, Tiffany & Co. New York, ca. 1910.
Graphic Arts Ephemera Collection.

Slat puzzle picture, chromolithograph, Milton Bradley Co. Springfield, Massachusetts, ca. 1905. Graphic Arts Ephemera Collection.

GAMES AND TOYS

Indoor card, puzzle and board games, like so many pleasant Victorian pastimes, have almost vanished in the late twentieth century. Home entertainment has sadly yielded, like private reading, to the easy lure of television. Old playing cards have also become a significant part of printed ephemera, and have traversed all periods and styles in their making. Their printed imagery is amazingly durable rather than ephemeral, with the face cards antique King, Queen, and Knave somehow frozen in time since the fifteenth century, despite efforts to dethrone them. Even the French Revolution, with a new design of *Citoyen* face cards, or the American revolution with Presidents as kings, did little to dislodge the royal family from the face cards of traditional card packs. A fascinating variant form of playing cards are the *jeux d'esprit* designs known as Transformation Cards. With such cards, the number pips (hearts, spades, clubs and diamonds) are made over into clever pictures and the face cards given startling new expressions not usually associated with regal imagery.

Other printed games far more familiar to another generation are jigsaw puzzles and board games. The Victorian imagination developed a splendid array of highly graphic games from *Abcedaires* and alphabet blocks for teaching the ABC's to such pictorial ingenuities as cube and slat pictures, *Myrioramas*, or horizon-joined, infinitely rearrangeable landscape strips, Panoramas, or long landscape scrolls, miniature peep-shows, and paper dolls. All are fragile reminders of a more innocent age. All were calculated to make learning a delight rather than a drudge. Related to these richly graphic toys are the optical toys now important as highly collectible non-paper ephemera. These include such pleasant mechanical apparatus as the Kaleidoscope, the Stereoscope, and the many elaborately named toy ancestors of Moving Pictures: the Magic Lantern, the Phenakistoscope, the Fantascope, and the *ZOETROPE* (q.v.).

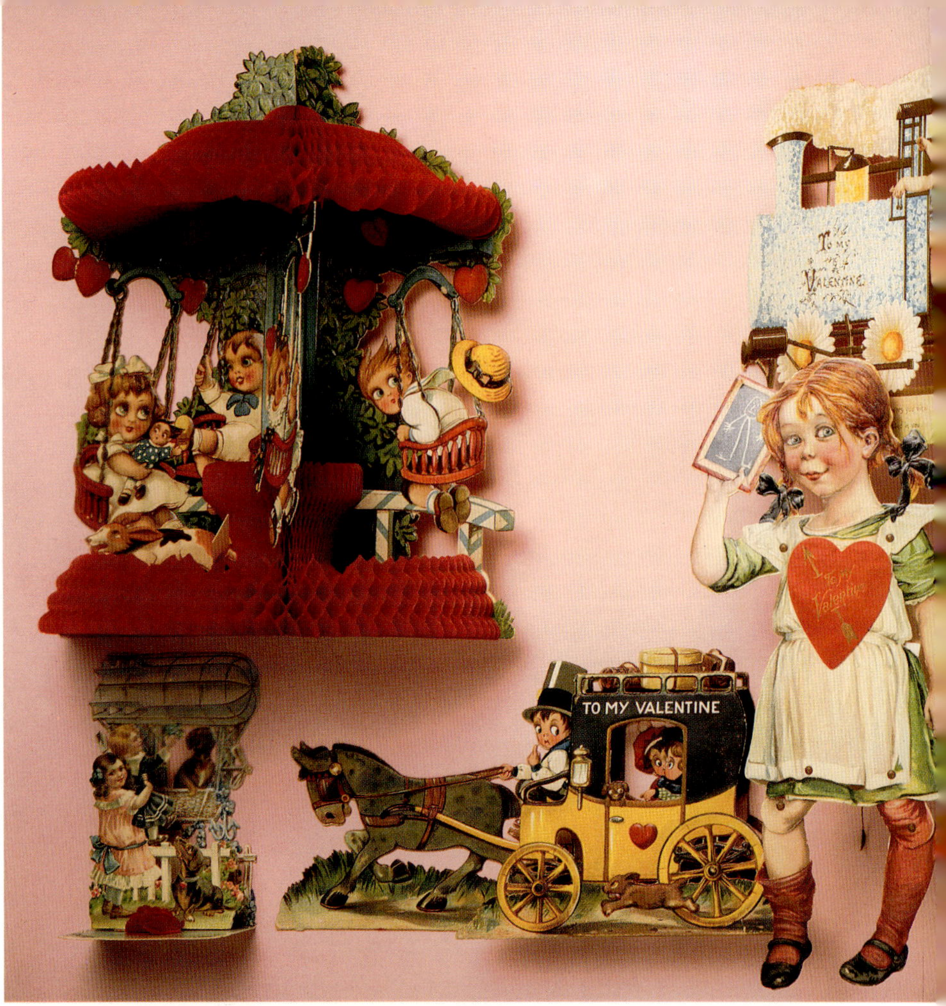

VALENTINES
FOR THE
MILLION!
At 144 Merrimack St.

The subscriber has just received from New York and Boston, a general assortment of

VALENTINES,

Amusing and affecting; beautiful and bewitching; comical and capital; delicate and delightful; elegant and entertaining; fantastic and funny; grave and gay; handsome and humorous; incomparable and inexpressible; jocose and jovial; killing and knowing; lively and laughable; merry and magnificent; neat and nice; ornamental and overwhelming; panegyrical and pantomimical; queer and quizzical; refreshing and romantic; serious and sentimental; tender and tasteful; unique and utile; valuable and veritable; witty and wonderful; xtensive and xtraordinary, &c.

Also, VALENTINE WRITERS, ENVELOPES, LACE PAPERS, etc. etc.

☞ **Please call and examine.**

JAMES P. WALKER,
144 *Merrimack St.*

B. H. PENHALLOW, PRINTER, Wyman's Exchange

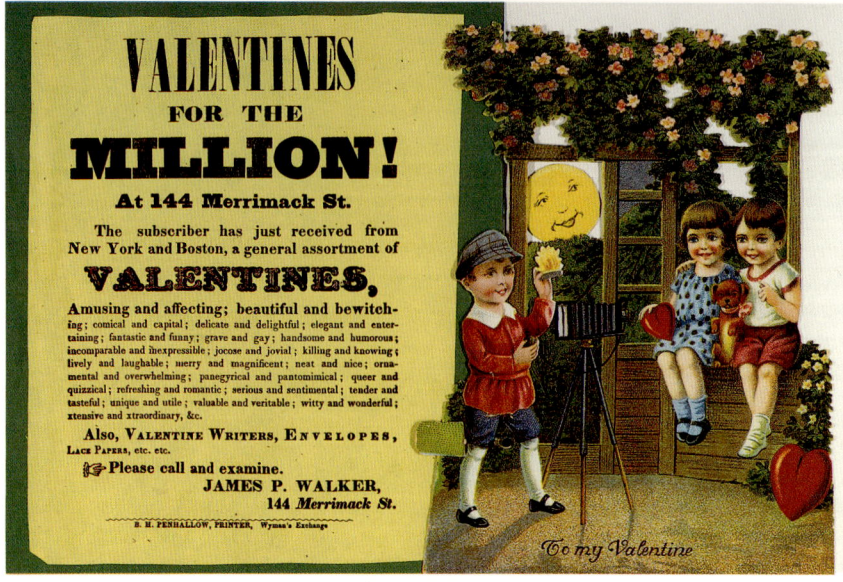

Valentine moveable, chromolithograph, B.H. Penhallow. N.p., n.d. Lent by Jack Golden. (A tab pull makes the moon rise as the photographer takes the picture.)

Selected Greeting Cards. Lent by Jack Golden.

GREETING CARDS

Prime among the many nineteenth century developments in color printed ephemera was the phenomenon of the greeting card. While the idea of New Year's, Christmas and St. Valentines celebration was already very old, the printed card for these holidays suddenly became the epitome of high Victorian fashion. An unparalleled appetite for unabashedly pretty decoration brought new developments of chromolithography, embossment, lacepapers, diecuts and a whole new fulsome repertoire for the printing arts. The decoration was at first done at home as a pleasant form of rainy day recreation, but under the later entrepreneurship of the Boston printer Louis Prang became a major industry. It was a golden age both for sentimental feeling and printed embellishments. When found in good condition with movable parts or three dimensional cutouts, with lace papers or bordered with that ultimate Victorian adornment, the silk fringe, greeting cards may be the most charming of paper antiques. The entire graphic repertoire of greeting cards is also to be found in *NOVELTY CARDS* (q.v.) and in specialty *POST CARDS* (q.v.).

Naval Cap Ornaments, early color lithograph, Peter Duval. Philadelphia, 1852. Graphic Arts, Sinclair Hamilton Collection. Selection of illustrated buttons lent by Jack Golden.

INSIGNIA, BADGES, AND BUTTONS

The chevrons and stripes of military uniforms are good examples of an unexpected type of more formal ephemera, both in meaning and materials used. The cloth patches of insignia give instant authority and level of command to the wearer, and become a very significant part of the military uniform. But the power and glory is eventually ephemeral, and the insignia, while effective as graphic emblem, are really only a passing show. While not collected in the same way as have been military medals and badges, woven insignia make up an excellent display in their own right, free from all the moral conflict, discipline, and frequent misery more truly associated with most wartime pursuits. Related to insignia as dress embellishment is the surprising but extensive ephemera genre of printed buttons. The discovery of celluloid led to its use in many inventive ways, including buttons and pocket mirror backs. Badges and buttons also make up a rich segment of the blazing chauvinism of political ephemera.

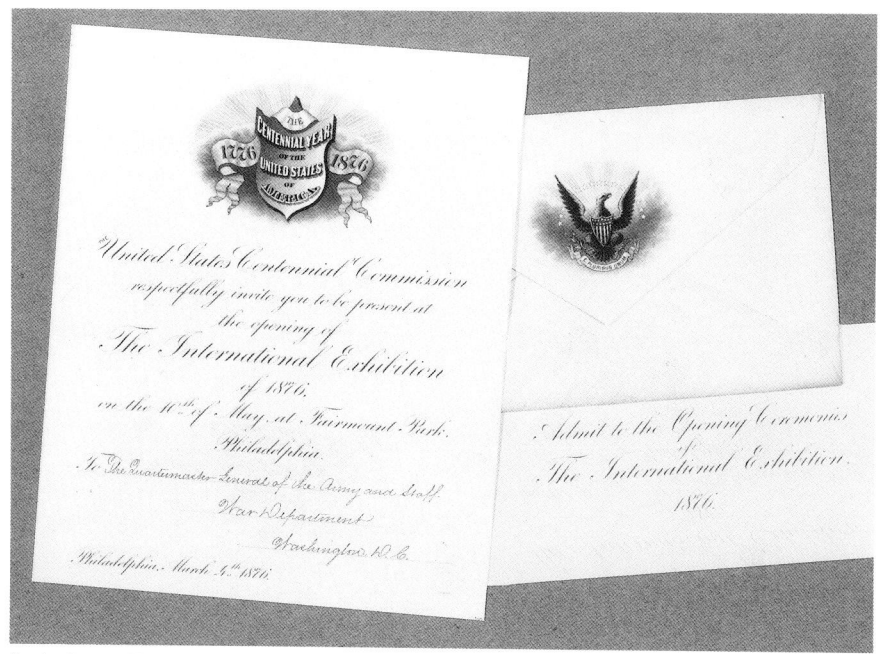

Invitation to The International Exhibition, engraving, artist unknown. Philadelphia, 1876. Lent by Jack Golden.

INVITATIONS

A printed personal invitation is a curious class of fugitive ephemera loaded with meaning out of all proportion to its diminutive size. R.S.V.P. invitations may be particularly unsettling in that deliberation, decision and action are quickly demanded of the recipient. An entire hierarchy of levels of the social scale is also often involved, and of course the questions of obligation, reciprocation and other responsibilities are mixed with the anticipation of merely having a good time. The design of invitations is a matter of very wide choice, from the formal dignity of an engraved wedding invitation to the informal boozy implications of a BYOB cocktail party card. Formal invitations may also involve the most elaborate protocol for official dinners, or merely a form of announcement for the opening of an exhibition.

Flatiron Building with perforated windows, chromolithograph, J. Kohler.
New York, 1920. Graphic Arts Ephemera Collection.

NOVELTY CARDS AND HOLD-TO-LIGHTS

A creative spin-off of the surge in printed ephemera of the nineteenth century
was in new ideas about how to use paper, print, and cardboard. The most
ingenious of these paper tricks included cutouts, foldouts, metamorphoses,
hold-to-lights, pull-outs, and movables, including rotating "grommet" cards and
pop-ups. Some of these paper engineering devices had antiquarian prototypes,
including fold out maps, volvelles, and cutout anatomy charts but the nineteenth
century print trade developed all of these novelty forms to new, unprecedented
levels of popularity and ingenuity. Some of the most interesting types are
described here.

Hold-to-Lights have an interesting history, and have always been a special
delight to view. The principles of opacity and transparency are exploited, with
pin pricks through the print to create actual points of light when held up against
a light source, and use of thinner paper layers to create transparent color, as in
stained glass. Such *Vue d'optique* prints enjoyed great popularity in the
eighteenth century. Edward Orme wrote *An Essay on Transparent Prints,*
published in London in 1807, which describes the use of varnish to create
wonderful effects of transparency where desired in a print. A special viewing
box called the Megalithoscope was invented later by one Carlo Ponti, of Venice,
to view transparencies and pin-pricked prints. The same ideas are found, to the
collector's delight, in certain nineteenth century trade cards and postcards,
which can light up like a Christmas tree when held up to the light.

The White House, chromolithograph, Gast Lithography. New York, ca. 1890. Lent by Jack Golden. (The card folds out, showing the White House outside and inside, where the product is advertised in the White House Kitchen.)

NOVELTY METAMORPHOSES AND MOVABLES

The *Foldout* has enough established history to review it briefly here. Foldout prints first appeared in a 15th century book, Breydenbach's *Peregrinations*, printed in 1483 in Mainz. This celebrated incunabulum contains foldout woodcuts with panoramic views of the Holy Land and an extraordinary multifold panorama of Venice. In the eighteenth century a new variation of the foldout evolved with a toy like print called a *Harlequinade*, invented by one Robert Sawyer, with divided flaps to change the picture from man to woman, or dog to cat, or whatever the print contained. In the nineteenth century, the form evolved into foldouts called *metamorphoses*, or transformations, which opened up to reveal the before and after effects of using the product. The idea of "before and after" would become an endless advertising staple of the next century. Metamorphosis prints also often represent narrative time, an element curiously often related in meaning to ephemera. Foldouts also realized the potential for depicting the third dimension of depth by anatomical foldout paper mannequins, found in certain nineteenth century medical dictionaries.

Movables, *pull-outs*, and *pop-ups* were developed by a German artist of great imagination and wit, Lothar Meggendorfer. His extraordinary color books for children include all sorts of paper engineering tricks that make his delightful drawings spring to life like some Victorian clockwork. The secret involves paper strips that are attached to grommet pins so that, when the tabs are pulled, many parts of the picture move. The grommet, or metal eyelet, was a fastening device used for many movables, from which a second underlying card was rotated. Meggendorfer's influence created a vast graphic ephemera progeny that includes any number of movable and pop-up Victorian Valentines, trade cards, and a more recently expanded area of collectibles, pop-up books.

Tiger Matches, color woodcut, J. Eaton and Son. N.p., 1879. Graphic Arts Ephemera Collection.

PACKAGING

When a number of layers of paper are pasted together and pressed flat, cardboard results. The development of the use of this tougher material resulted in cardboard boxes and cartons, and the vast realm of cardboard packaging was born. The ephemeral essence of nineteenth century packaging was well expressed by Alphaeus Hyatt Mayor, then print curator of the Metropolitan Museum, when he remarked, "Anyone can find a Whistler etching but just try and find a Victorian match box." Packaging *Wrappers* of all sorts are instant throwaways. Only the most ardent ephemerist, such as Princeton's own Frederic Fox, Class of 1939, would create a collection of candy wrappers. His collection of 30s and 40s candy packaging, now in Firestone Library's Graphic Arts Collection, is prime nostalgia for the undergraduate classes of those years.

Band Box. N.p., ca. 1840. Lent by the Buccleuch Mansion, New Brunswick, N. J. (Once owned by Margaret Beckman-Vanderbilt.)

PACKAGING - BOXES

The earliest of American packaging is well represented by the eighteenth century hat box known as a band box. Such boxes involved a very decorative overlay of block printed and pasted paper strips of early American wall papers. By the 1820s this uniquely American treatment gave the mundane storage box an elegant look all its own. Often using the sleek shape of the oval Shaker box design with full color block prints as highly decorative wrappers, the American band box not only became a fashionable necessity but entered the language as an easy gallantry: "as pretty as a band box." Not so pretty is the later American consumer over-dependence on cardboard boxing, which contributes enormously to our growing man-made mountains of modern waste.

Selected Cigar Box Art. Lent by Jack Golden.

The Celebrated Fashion, early tobacco box color lithograph, Louis Rosenthal. Philadelphia, ca. 1850. Graphic Arts Ephemera Collection.

PACKAGING - CIGAR BOX ART

Decorating boxes to define contents gradually became an American advertising specialty from the early band box to our own time, when pictorial boxing has become a gargantuan printing industry. A significant phase of this specialty boxing was the American and Cuban cigar box. Neatly crafted in wood, these cigar boxes are highly collectable, particularly when embellished with a pasted chromolithograph label calculated to outshine all other paper labels. Embossed and elaborately printed in the most garish colors and gold, these labels created an ephemera art all their own. There were series named after the Gods of Rome, Old Dutch Masters, and the Plays of Shakespeare, all as lurid as the printer could make them. To save on offcut printing, cigar bands were printed and placed on every cigar. These gold paper rings, like cigar box covers, are also still collected.

Linen labels, color lithograph and embossment. Philadelphia, ca. 1850. Lent by Jack Golden.

PACKAGING - LABELS

The affixing of a printed label to the front of a container has such sound logic that it is surprising that the idea was not exploited sooner. Shapes of liquor bottles, not labels, once designated contents, square for gin, round for brandy, etc., just as they still do for crystal decanters. Printers' labels took hold only when it was realized that they could both advertise and visually imply the quality of the product. *Linen Labels* were among the first paper labels to proliferate as a type. Done mainly in the 1840s and 50s to identify yard goods, linen labels are unusually beautiful examples of early American color printing, embossment, and printing in gold and silver. Another early label development was for dividing packages of hand paper. Known as *Ream Wrappers*, these often offer fine woodcut pictures of some of our first paper mills. Later labels with collecting categories all their own are *Liquor Labels, Canning Labels* and *Orange Crate Labels*.

World Columbian Exhibition Postcards, color lithograph, Charles Goldsmith. Chicago, 1893. Graphic Arts Ephemera Collection.

POST CARDS

The postcard was first introduced in England in 1839 as a postal message card to be delivered without envelope. Such cards were not used in America until 1873, when the Government Post Office finally offered 3 x 5 1/8 inch cards, watermarked USPOD at the cost of one cent each. Picture postcards did not follow until 1893 when the American Souvenir Company of Boston's picture cards appeared. American picture postcards before 1898, however, are rare. As the cheapest and laziest of personal message devices ("Wish you were here"), the penny postcard proliferated beyond all bounds. Highly inventive variations of the form make several fascinating categories of their own, including *Hold-to-Lights* and *EMBOSSMENTS* (q.v.). Postcard collectors emerged early on, Queen Victoria among them, and Deltiology, or Cartophilia, as collecting postcards is known, is a major pursuit to this day.

Selected Postcard folders. Lent by Jack Golden.

POST CARD FOLDERS

The simple device of binding picture postcard strips together by folding represents a late variation on an ancient form. The earliest oriental format as well as the classical codex were actually similar folders made from a long strip or scroll. Now called "accordion" or "concertina" style, such folding inspired the America travel folders of preprinted postcards that became standard travel souvenirs of the 1930's. These cheaply printed folders gave extra printing mileage for postcards of almost every town of any self-respect throughout America. A Civil War prototype was the "Union Rose" accordion souvenir folder. Another graphic prototype of the postcard folder were the late Victorian travel folders issued by the Witteman Brothers in New York. Usually drawn by one Louis Glaser in lithographic reduction after photographs, these early accordion fold pictures often have a surreal atmosphere and mood combined with an amazing sharpness of detail. They offer superior quality both in art and technique to the smudged color banality so evident in later color postcards.

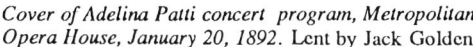

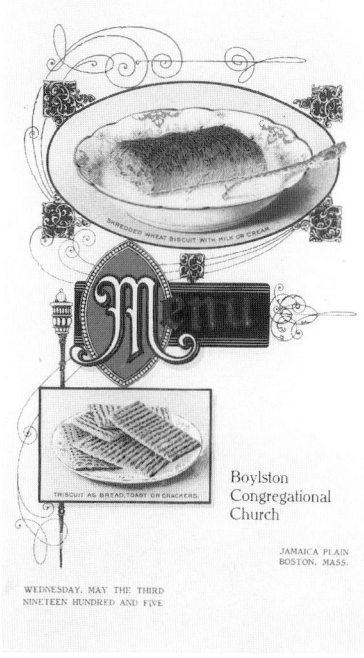

Boylston
Congregational
Church

Cover of Adelina Patti concert program, Metropolitan
Opera House, January 20, 1892. Lent by Jack Golden.

Boylston Congregational Church Menu,
chromolithograph, artist unknown. Boston,
Massachusetts, 1905. Lent by Jack Golden.

PROGRAMS AND MENUS

Like the calendar, programs are the essence of ephemera, being records of what
happened at a particular time and place, and never to happen quite in the same
way again. Old concert and theater programs also reveal surprising shifts of
cultural taste, both in choice and degree of sophistication. The extreme length
of early concerts always comes as a shock to modern concert goers, as does the
number of forgotten composers. Even more quickly forgotten are the
performers and actors of old concert and theater productions, so that old printed
playbills and programs often offer documentation of the history of music and
drama to be found nowhere else. Menus for restaurants may be classed as
programs for eating. Souvenir menus are usually the only ones to survive, but
early examples of ordinary menus are fascinating as documents of taste and
change in diet habits. Like calendars, menus are both quotidian essentials and
ephemera throwaways. Menu cover art is usually minimal, but some help
arouse the diner's appetite with savory depictions of the menu's great *raison
d'etre*, food. This elaborate pictorial example for the Boylston Congregational
Church turns out sparse offerings.

Selected Rewards of Merit. Lent by Alfred Malpa.

REWARDS OF MERIT

Slips of paper printed with acknowledgement of the recipient's good behavior may be said to go back all the way to the earliest printing, in the fifteenth century, of papal indulgences. A similar but much later use of printed acknowledgement of meritorious behavior appeared in the late eighteenth century and early nineteenth century America with a printed "reward of merit" for good children. A kind of pictorial report card, these little printed tokens inscribed for "a good girl" or "A good Scholar" gave a vicarious pat on the head to those just learning to read, and a clear moral message of the importance of being good.

Cigarette Cards, uncut proof chromolithograph on silk. Graphic Arts Ephemera Collection.

SERIES CARDS

The powerful instinct to collect more of a "set", whether it be furniture, dishes, or printed things of a similar kind, was recognized almost at once by early American advertisers. Cigarette cards and baseball cards have flourished along with their tobacco product as examples of this basic compulsion. Tobacco selling exploited every aspect of such printing and packaging, from the cigar box (see *PACKAGING*) to the first naughty show-girl insert cards. Another bad habit product, bubble gum, was also marketed with baseball cards, still among the most artificially elevated and sought after of trade cards. Earlier series cards were almost always issued in tidy sets of six, many of which are delightful as proto-comic strips. Among the most artistically desirable, however, are Louis Prang chromolithographic sets such as Central Park, and other early American scenery sets.

47

Window display screen for Coca-Cola, the Year Round Drink, color lithograph, artist unknown. N.p., n.d. Lent by Jack Golden.

SHOW CARDS

A variation on the *BROADSIDE* and *POSTER* forms, *SHOW CARDS* represent a more creative aspect of advertising art. Designed to be a large window or instant counter display, showcards are like small portable billboards turned into folding triptychs, folding screens or flat cutouts with a back stand attached. Show cards, as their name implies, were the high art of printed ephemera advertising, with the most visually ambitious imagery the commercial artist could devise. Many are very frameworthy and a few are masterpieces of the genre. Coca-Cola employed some of the best of such painters, well seen in this extremely fine five-fold screen representing " the pause that refreshes" in all seasons.

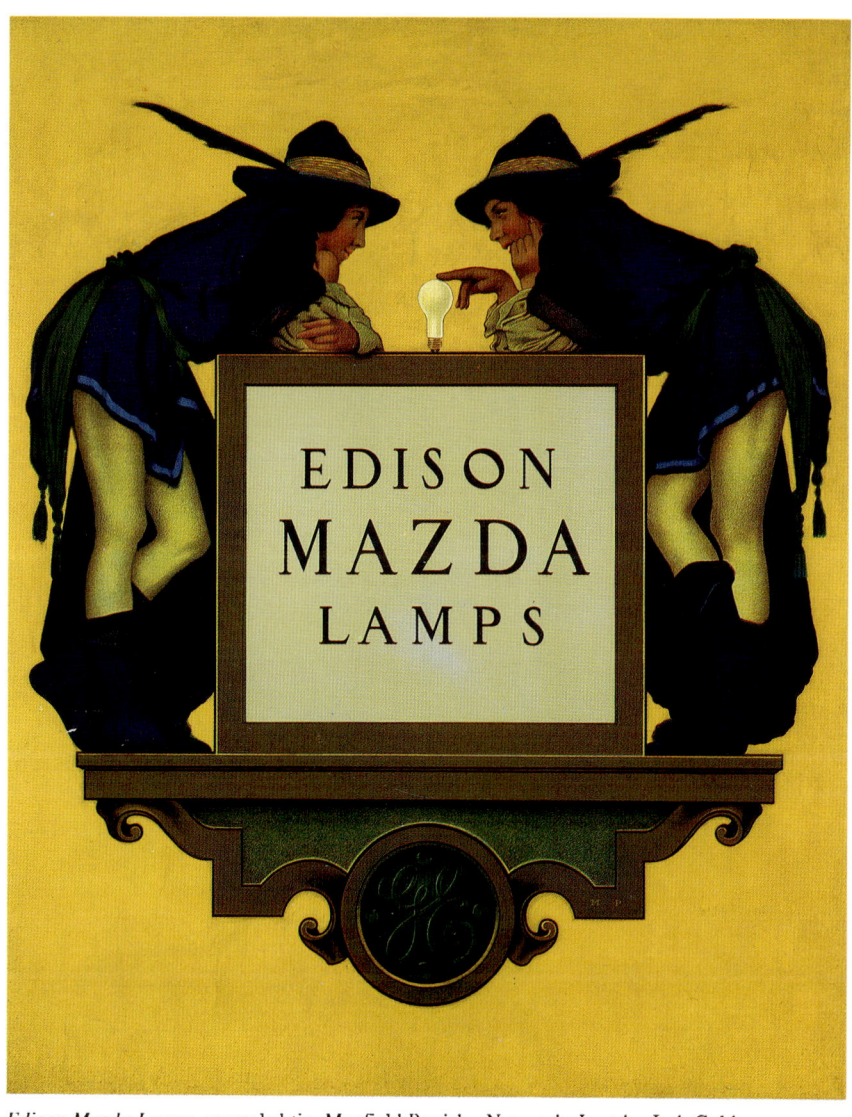

Edison Mazda Lamps, enameled tin, Maxfield Parrish. N.p., n.d. Lent by Jack Golden.

SIGNS

Like showcards, signs inspired some of the early designers' best efforts. More lasting than most ephemera, since they are usually not on paper but painted on wood or enameled on metal, good signs have the desirability of both hardy construction and sculptural presence. Early American tavern and hanging shop signs have become very rare and valuable as antiques. Some were even painted by such eminent artists as Benjamin West, Gilbert Stuart and Edward Hicks. A 1920s revival of the hanging shop sign was created by Maxfield Parrish with his brilliantly enameled tin signs for Edison Mazda Lamps. Enameled or transfer lithograph signs on metal are known as "Advertising Tins" among ephemera collectors.

Selected illustrated envelopes. Lent by Jack Golden.

STATIONERY-ENVELOPES

Now taken for granted, envelopes go back as far as ancient Babylonian cuneiform tablets, when an outer clay covering was baked around the terracotta message inside. Paper envelopes, like their remote ancestor, give an essential protection and privacy to any record or message. In the last century, the envelope's further potential as image vehicle was soon realized, and illustrated covers became commonplace. Simple corner-illustrated covers, printed in red and blue, were popular in the Civil War.

Selected Letterheads. Lent by Jack Golden.

STATIONERY-LETTERHEADS

Distinctive typographic and pictorial letterheads and bill-heads combined the graphic communication of the business card and direct mail advertising. By the beginning of the twentieth century, every firm of any stature had its own image established at the top of all correspondence by its own letterhead design. The practice was a bonanza for the local job printer, particularly when rival firms started to outdo one another in the use of ever more fancy pictorial motifs and multicolor printing. The early distributors of motion pictures and circus managers Barnum and Bailey had printed the most lavish of early American letterheads, selling their image not only in barnside posters but in every sheet of correspondence.

Tickets for medical students, engravings, Peter Maverick. New York, ca. 1826. Lent by William Helfand.

TICKETS

The perfect example of ephemera, tickets are momentarily essential for admission, but soon lose their importance, torn in half and saved only temporarily as a stub or, equally demeaning, violated by the ticket punch. Old tickets, when they are by chance preserved, do have their own graphic charm as some of the smallest of printed ephemera. In the eighteenth and early nineteenth century they were often finely engraved, a technique seen in these rare early tickets for medical student admission to the operating theater of Rutgers Medical College. Early lottery tickets are also of special interest as are circus and minstrel show tickets and passes. Railroad, boating, theater and opera also represent ticket genre all their own with very limited survival rates.

 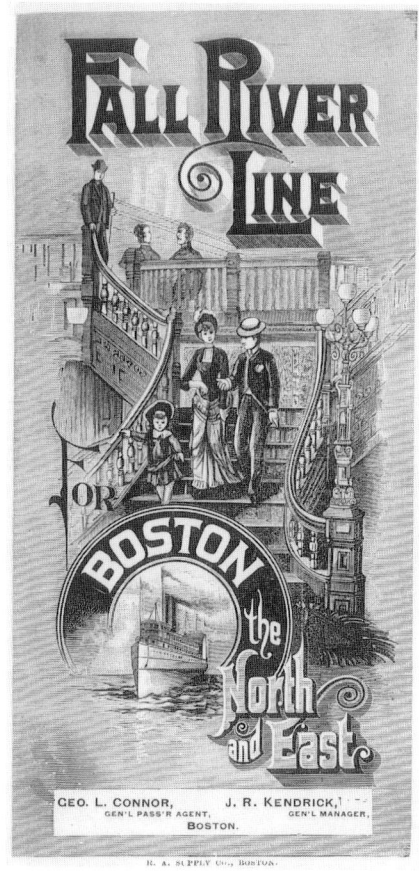

Railroad and Ship Timetables, letterpress, artists unknown. N.p., n.d. Lent by Paul Ingersoll.

TIMETABLES

Another perfect example of throwaway printed ephemera is the travel timetable. The tall pocket size format was established early, and both railroad departures and ship sailing listings were constantly recharted and readjusted for the traveler's easier understanding. Reading timetables however, still confuses some travelers. It is the pictorial covers, however, that offer the most graphic interest in old timetables and often inspire intense nostalgia for both railroad and boat travel. The loss is specially felt for such great vanished pleasure boats as the old Fall River Line between Boston and New York and, saddest of all, the great ocean liners to Europe.

Selected trade cards. Graphic Arts Ephemera Collection.

Flying Scud, color woodcut, Nesbitt and Co. New York, ca. 1855. Lent by Jack Golden.

TRADE CARDS

America saw its first nationwide manifestation of strategic advertising in a flood of small 3 x 5 inch cards, or trade cards, chromolithographed in full color, and given out to customers in great quantity and extraordinary variety during the last decades of the nineteenth century. The idea for such cards goes back to European tradesmen of the seventeenth and eighteenth century, who handed out small engraved cards to associates and customers as a printed name, address, and wares reminder. These early English cards, often beautifully engraved, have become rare, true collector's items, and offer a glimpse of trade in eighteenth century London as an elegant, more class aware way of marketing. In contrast, the American version of such cards opened the first great floodgate of democratic advertising. Color, preposterous claims, ubiquity through huge printing numbers, and a new energized hucksterism turned the genteel English trade card into an early American advertising free-for-all. American trade cards may also be said to follow in another European tradition, Books of Trades and Street Cries, with depiction of every variety of new American trades and products. We also find rich early imagery of such modern concerns as city and country, rich and poor, as well as nineteenth century roles of women and minorities. Arranged by iconographic subdivision, trade cards present a picture book of America in the last century like no other. Among the rarest and most graphic of early American trade cards was a distinct genre known as *CLIPPER SHIP CARDS*, announcing the sailing time of Clipper ships, usually from Boston and New York to San Francisco. Clipper ship cards are distinguished for their precisely printed, zestful imagery in letterpress and color woodcut on a glossy cardboard surface. The combination of extreme rarity and decorative quality place clipper cards among the most valuable of printed ephemera. They are also excellent examples of very early American color printing.

Yellow Rose Theorem Painting and Seed Packet Covers from early garden catalogues. Graphic Arts Ephemera Collection. *Selected Trade Catalogues.* Lent by Jack Golden.

TRADE CATALOGUES

The American trade card success soon led to a more serious advertising of wares for sale through small bound paperbacks showing customers a series of pictures of available merchandise. Covering almost every aspect of American daily life from farm machinery and tools to coal stoves and sewing machines, these catalogues were issued in large editions, and were usually profusely illustrated with technically adept woodengravings of the product. Later "Mail Order" catalogues became a big business for Sears and many others. Appearing at a time of rapid industrial growth, the catalogues not only documented a rapidly expanding country, but reveal a new boastful pride in American goods and services as the best in the world. Among the most attractive forms of trade catalogues were the Nurserymen or Garden Seed Catalogues. Color printing has fine display here, from early American theorem painting (a form of stencil), to rich chromolithography for both catalogue and seed packet. Mailed out in the midst of winter, beautifully illustrated spring flower catalogues have always found an enthusiastic market.

Victor Talking Machine Co., chromolithograph, artist unknown. Camden, New Jersey, 1904. Lent by Jack Golden.

TRADEMARKS

The idea of a graphic symbol to identify a product grew up along with the trade card and the burgeoning progression of advertising as a major part of merchandising. Few emblems are as long remembered as the spotted dog listening to "his Master's voice" to identify the new Victor Talking Machine or Victrola. It was an age of new American inventions, all of which are to be found in pictures in trade cards and early advertising art. Besides the phonograph, Otis elevators, Singer Sewing machines, the telephone, gas light, the bicycle, the typewriter and other inventions find their first images on late nineteenth century trade cards. Commercial art soon followed as an artistic profession to become an essential co-conspirator in promotion and selling by both image and product.

The Spencerian Pen Co., printed card with actual steel nibs, artist unknown. New York, n.d. Graphic Arts Ephemera Collection, Gift of Allen Scheuch.

TRADE SAMPLE CARDS AND BOOKS

Small ephemeral treasures are wonderfully represented by those occasional cards and booklets containing actual samplings of the product. These include paint-chip cards and books, thread and ribbon catalogues, textiles and wall paper samples, as well as salesmen's dummy's of sample bookbindings and even greeting cards available for sale. Such original bits of Victorian archaeology are individual clues to taste and sociology of their period, offering both primary research evidence of the first order along with their original packaged documentation.

58

Souvenir trays for various products, transfer print on tin, C. W. Shonk Lithography. Chicago, n.d.
Lent by Jack Golden.

TRADE TINWARE

The phenomenal success of the trade card as early advertising inspired a number of variant non-paper printed wares. Textiles, the newly invented celluloid as well as tin were all used for often elaborate advertising presentation. Highly collectible today are the inventive tins from the 1870s onward in England and America for biscuits and cookies, with their transfer printed patterns. More direct advertising is to be found in a series of tin trays made for such nearly forgotten beverages as Stegmaier Beer, Moxie, and the still thriving Coca-Cola. In addition to trays, decorated buttons, mirrors, and a myriad variety of other objects were produced in both tin and celluloid.

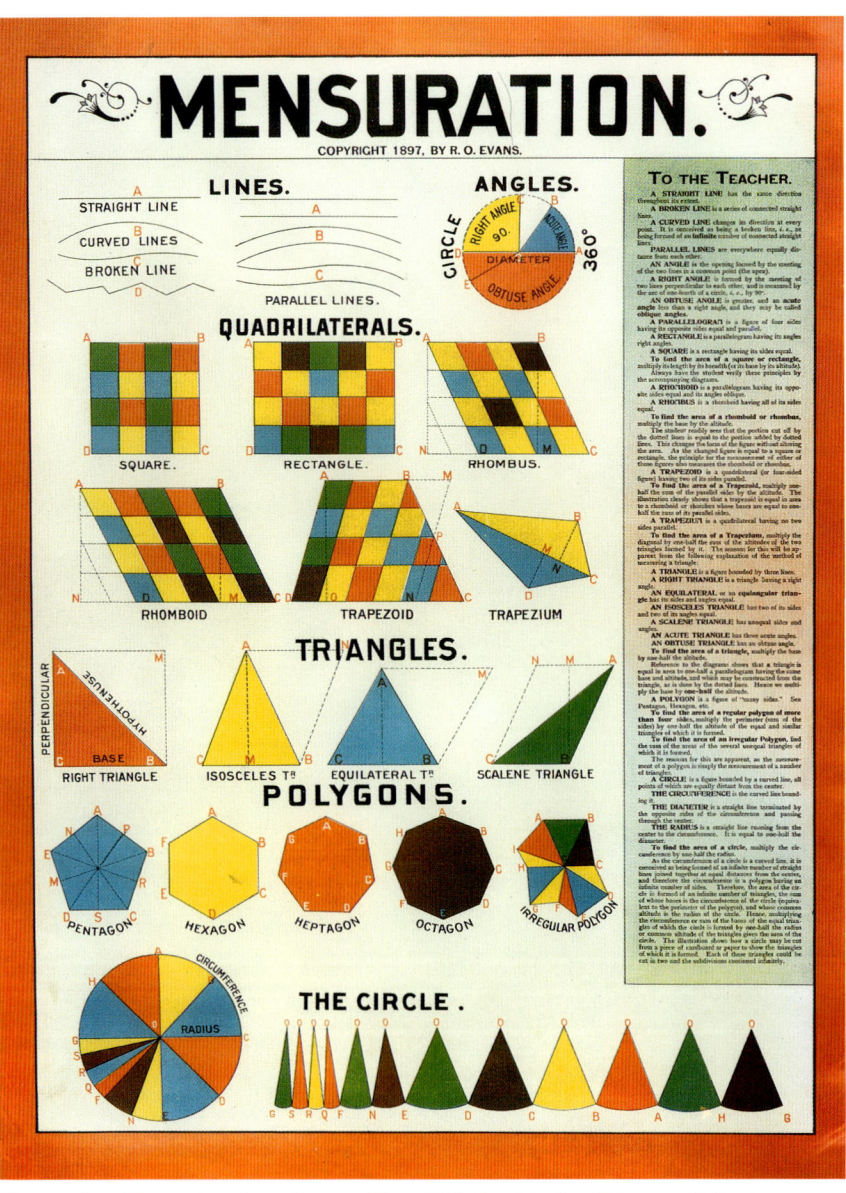

Mensuration, lithograph, artist unknown. N.p., 1897, Graphic Arts Ephemera Collection.

Wall Chart from Louis Prang's "Aids for Object Teaching." Boston, 1874. Graphic Arts Collection.

WALL CHARTS

Classroom decoration in American elementary schools usually included a print of Stuart's portrait of Washington and assorted wall charts of widely varying complexity. Prang issued a famous series of "Aids for Object Teaching" for children that gives an American update for the *Orbis Pictus* or world in pictures for children of earlier centuries in Europe. Richard O. Evans issued a much more challenging series of educational wall charts in 1897, teaching young scholars such subjects as mensuration, or applied geometry, the metric system and percentages, in what seems to be a somewhat naive belief that bright colors and pictures will make these fearsome subjects easy.

Printed watchpaper. Paterson, N.J., 1852. Lent by the Trenton State Historical Museum.

WATCHPAPERS

Another example of printed ephemera closely linked to passing time, these small printed paper inserts were placed in pocket watches to protect the inner works from dust. They also made a charming and convenient advertisement for the maker or repairer of watches, much as furniture-maker labels or frame maker-labels were attached to the product involved. Such maker's labels, when in place, have become invaluable in the documentation of antiques. Attached to an eighteenth century high-boy or fine grandfather clock, what might have been an ephemeral label becomes a zealously preserved miniature document.

Jack in the Box, zoetrope strip, hand-colored engraving. N.p., n.d. Graphic Arts Ephemera Collection.

ZOETROPES

The beginning of moving pictures is linked to a variety of early experimental toys that exploited the phenomenon of the persistence of vision. The first of these was the *ZOETROPE*, developed in 1833. A series of printed cartoons, each slightly different, was created as zoetrope paper strips and placed inside a revolving slotted drum. When the viewer looked through one of the slots and the drum revolved, the drawings moved. These zoetrope strips were the ancestors of animated cartoon cells and mark the graphic beginning of an entire new era of communication. Both surviving zoetrope strips and the modern cartoon cells that evolved from them must be regarded as a class of ephemera, neglected until recent years by collectors. As a San Francisco paper (*Alta* May 4, 1889) so prophetically said of Eadweard Muybridge and his *zoopraxiscope*, the photographic equivalent of the *ZOETROPE,* "here is the foundation of a new method of entertaining the people."

GRAPHIC EPHEMERA FORMS · ABECEDAIRES TO ZOETROPES

Catalogue designed by Jack Golden,
Designers 3, Inc.

Trompe L'Oeil cover designed by
Greg Smart, Dale Roylance and Allen Scheuch.

Typography for text set in Times Roman
by Agnes Sherman and Matthew Robb.

Photography by Clem Fiori.

Title page wood engraving from the
James Connors Sons
1870 Type Specimen Catalogue.

Warren's Lustro Offset Dull,
80 lb. text and 80 lb. cover papers
were chosen for the production
of this catalogue.

Color separations and printing by
Fleetwood Fine Arts.

Binding by Intergraphic Bindery.